# THE INSIDE OF A STONE

**Charlotte Van den Broeck** was born in Turnhout, Belgium, in 1991. After studies in English and German, she took a Masters in Drama at the Royal Conservatoire in Antwerp. She has published three collections of poetry, *Kameleon* (2015), which was awarded the Herman de Coninck debut prize for poetry by a Flemish author; *Nachtroer* (2017), which was nominated for the VSB Poetry Prize 2018 and the Ida Gerhard Prize; and *Aarduitwrijvingen* (2021). The first two volumes are combined in *Chameleon | Nachtroer*, translated from the Dutch by David Colmer (Bloodaxe Books, 2020). This collection, David Colmer's translation of *Aarduitwrijvingen*, was first published by Bloodaxe in 2025 under the title *The Inside of a Stone*. Her poetry has also been translated into German, Spanish, French, Serbian and Arabic.

In 2016 she opened the Frankfurt Bookfair together with Dutch author Arnon Grunberg. In 2017 she was one of that year's Verso-polis poets, performing at several European festivals including Ledbury in Britain. In 2022 David McKay's translation of her prose book *Bold Ventures: Thirteen Tales of Architectural Tragedy* (Waagstukken) was published by Chatto in the UK and by Other Press in the US. As well as publishing critically acclaimed books she is renowned for her distinctive performances, which differ from UK/US versions of spoken word as theatre pieces 'searching for the speakability and experience of oral poetry', now presented in English as well as Dutch.

# Charlotte Van den Broeck

# THE INSIDE
# OF A STONE

translated by
DAVID COLMER

BLOODAXE BOOKS

ISBN:   978 1 78037 702 5

This translation published in the UK in 2025 by

Bloodaxe Books Ltd,

Eastburn,

South Park,

Hexham,

Northumberland NE46 1BS

**www.bloodaxebooks.com**
For further information about Bloodaxe titles
please visit our website and join our mailing list
or write to the above address for a catalogue.

This book was published with the support of Flanders Literature

Cover design: Neil Astley & Pamela Robertson-Pearce.

Printed in Great Britain by Bell & Bain Limited, Glasgow, Scotland, on
acid-free paper sourced from mills with FSC chain of custody certification.

all day I've built a lifetime
and now the sun sinks
to undo it

ANNE SEXTON: 'The Fury of Sunsets'

By returning to phenomena, we find, as a fundamental layer, a whole already pregnant with an irreducible sense. This is not a series of incomplete sensations between which memories would have to be embedded, but rather the physiognomy – the structure of the landscape or of the word – spontaneously in accordance with our present intentions and with our previous experience.

MAURICE MERLEAU-PONTY: *Phenomenology of Perception*, p. 23
(tr. Donald A. Landes)

The preparatory study for this collection took place in the context of the research project *aarduitwrijvingen / peak* at the Royal Conservatoire Antwerp (2019–21) in close dialogue with the work of audio-visual artist Jana Coorevits. I cherish our mutual metaphor linking body and landscape and our many conversations about it.

# CONTENTS

| | | | |
|---|---|---|---|
| 9 | immersion | 28 | hiss |
| 10 | damaged | 29 | sketch |
| 11 | migraine | 30 | on the pond |
| 12 | vulture | 35 | in the bog |
| 13 | inside of a stone | 36 | remedies |
| 14 | thief | 37 | history of gemstones |
| 15 | the large and small snake goddesses | 38 | aphrodite of knidos (360 BC) |
| 16 | scratchings | 41 | seismology |
| 17 | in a fold | 43 | tremors |
| 18 | phaethon | 44 | matar |
| 19 | road runner & wile e. coyote | 46 | terra preta |
| 21 | gouache | 49 | in memoriam |
| 22 | calcite | 50 | cholita |
| 23 | acting like stone like fruit | 52 | deformations |
| 24 | cone | 53 | on the reef |
| 25 | pulp | 54 | ilsebill dreams |
| 26 | acacia | 62 | seaview |
| 27 | wood anemone | | |

why do I see white as dismantled light
why do I refuse to believe what a perpendicular sun can do, even now
why is there no shadow under the sky, red orange red
the day igniting on repeat

why does the exhausted hour drag herself into focus, what is distance
if not an accumulating mass of sand – already chin high
why doesn't it come

to drowning even in her vastness
the wandering disintegrates

now with crescent shrubs, later from the dreamt sound
of a background motorway, rustling
where's that lizard rushing, why is the heat lisping

incantations, why do I pin my hopes
on the hidden tracks of nocturnal animals, the mirage
of an old love, why doesn't he call me – hasn't he lost me

immersion

the way I have been moving all this time
motionless while the wind shifts the sand

when night falls they say
the rocks walk

the desert tosses and turns, tugging her sheet
a woman

wakes undamaged, dresses
to go hiking, she doesn't lug ghosts

for miles
alone with the dazzle of sun and rock salt
alone with the vast retina

a blindness

because those who look into the light know
they have always been there
behind closed eyes, metallic shadows

climb into the bloodstream the stiffening light the light
deep in the white

eddying flash

dot throb blur, clotting
the landscape a zigzag mosaic
of headache a half skull

can someone cover the sun
can someone take away the spinning smells
the circular saw

when it comes

grip the ribs
guttural sounds wood shavings sediment
gall

the pounding thud the thump
that rips the skin of the sky a blended colour
gushing out anaesthetic

and pink breaking the iron-and-copper-rich
rock and purple the tick in the quartz
sings me to sleep

distance a certain form
of representation

perceptible as sound
detaching from the landscape
detaching from the dreamt
landscape from the curve

of the eye a chromatic dispersion
in the sparse crops and plants
white flecks
on the leaves of the date palms

circling
ascending learning

how the desert fox owes its age
to the vulture's hunger strike

in the bowl of the mountains
the dunes well up, eddies
in the sand, listening
to the secret parts

you see rocks, sharpness, the substance
but what you see is moving through it

blue and purple
the blood seeps
from the bowels of stone

for a while it felt like something might be salvageable
through a minimal exertion keeping
my body straight carrying myself
like a brimming glass to your lips, your lips

being made of water and letting myself be drunk
being someone's thirst, you did it

the way the creosote bush survives
by penetrating other roots with her roots
tapping into their reserves how else

can she preserve the green
in her waxy leaves
among all this death

too late the sap flows
before the snakebite shatters
the sand pours into the glass

stubbornly swinging their hips through the night
the large and small snake goddesses rake the desert
and every night again for centuries

combing the spirits out of the earth for us
while we sleep

fleeing the tines
shadowy ripples shoot over the sandy ridge
like something in the earth that's bare

and ready for sowing
constantly pursuing itself shivering
under the high sun averting evil
with an amulet

civilisations later when the goddesses
stand worn-out in disbelief
in a museum people

will leave their breasts uncovered
dismiss their task as snake charming

and something to do with fertility

through the cracks in the crust
moving up

a crystal shattering
the lie resounds
oscillating

on the surface the quaking
sand breaks

who deciphers the ground and her scratchings
who sleeps over there
in the shade of the mesquite

is he armed is it true
he wants to love you before you know it
you'll be a wounded person

of blood and salt and ruptures

at the base of the hill's throat the dip
in the waist of the reclining sand giant

asleep in the landscape the landscape hiding
in her, the tickling

wind plays with her beard of desert holly and silver
it smells bluish green, dull green, greenish
– gradually cooling a place to lie down and she lends you

her midriff she lends you her sleep a view
without footprints

primeval and plumped up
the bed spreads out the morning her body
a hospitable region, the folded layers

of rock you lie down in a hollow
and flow

a red word and the stars slide
you fly around an amply measured bend
further further

under your skin a herd of animals that can be designated horses
trotting to their watering place

the violence of hooves on marcasite
scarcely a spark further

more, inciting, not stopping
at the ruin of the tipped sun chariot onwards
a higher dawn, a steep climb

determined to trample itself underfoot of course
crashing down what did you expect
that a word of all things, red and truthful, would lift

you up out of the fall, that later the poplars
would cry as they are meant to cry
for the terrible burns for a boy guilty
of the origin of deserts

what can we learn about guile and fate

Road Runner leads the way in every episode, faster than a favourable wind, borne
by the script's doctrine of inevitability, in which, prior to each resurrection,
Coyote
must end in one or more of three ways:
>     burnt to a crisp
>     crushed, or
>     motionless on the canyon floor

followed by
standing up, vengeance

nobody knows what he's scheming now, but you can bet your bottom dollar:
armed to the teeth with tornado seeds gigantic catapults dehydrated boulders
and countless other gadgets, Coyote will not give up

because, as the artist apparently once said, it's not his dinner at stake
as much as his dignity

>     prairie wolf versus chaparral cock

a foregone struggle, one day his prey will be his, today

Wile E. Coyote is on an unfinished road
with a brush and a canvas cunningly he extends it out over the abyss
with three lifelike clouds, a crash barrier and a curve around the mountainside

– HEE HEE

DANGER! road stops here

19

BEEP BEEP
Road Runner comes racing up – BLURRED FEET
even if he saw the trap! he'd never stop in time!

     – HUNHH??? Road Runner doesn't plummet
     into the depths runs onto the canvas
     into the painting devising a loophole in the reign of might
     in the violent slapstick universe


running as far as thought can carry him through the painted landscape and in
this presentation of the imagined world there is no fall, no broken bones, no
predator to rip and devour him, completely astonished

Coyote scratches question marks out of his skull  SKRRRRR SKRRRRR not noticing
a truck racing at top speed out of the canvas – EEEEEEEEEEEK

CRRRKKKKKK-SPLTCH

but never dead for long

because according to a Warner Bros survey viewers sympathise
more with a brilliant never-say-die villain
than with a victim who successfully escapes

stand up

hunger, vengeance.

rain persists covering the sand
like a layer of gouache, a watercolour wash
of drab morass as if the landscape is

being painted over the landscape
with a mixture of gelatine, sludge and sepia

strolling through that canvas, drenched
and weary from searching, realising how past places
still wander through a body, deceitful

and seemingly fixed, an anamorphosis
of the remembered landscape that in no way

resembles this place I walked before, wet paint
constantly mixing with the unfaithful history
of clay soil, clastic, each step

absorbed by the ground and just as effortlessly
the prints let go again

presence, a streaming trail
I retrace and erase

drenched soil

pushes up stone that disintegrates
into thousands of pieces of calcite
anaemic glitter, how do you return

the defeated glow to the tired stars
body and wound

finally in harmony it's not possible the light
splits in the crystal doubly refracted

multiplied
you thought it was whole, clear, where

do the stone's coloured veins lead what
do the deposited minerals and fossil remnants

the calcified sea lily stalks
bear witness to

a woman feels sad
in her stomach
scraping a nectarine stone

she curls herself
around the innermost
in imitation of a fruit

keeps the cuckoo wasps at bay
grows

in the wide eye of noon
she really is hungry

but the fruit is hard
and bleeds on her gums

mint and resin how rain
whets a smell, tackiness

swelling the tear in the gingerbread bark
thickening the green in the tense needle
unstaunchable

colour gushing out
in a wash

of rain the woody cone opening
as its contracting scales
curl away with ripeness

sweet kiss of fermentation spoilage
lurking in the skin tongue
turning to lick the drupelets

blush colouring the fruit
and red spillage

the tooth craves and purple
cinches the berry

the rot
in your swollen mouth, biting, still

a word wakes expectation the evening
wakes the night she remains what she is

a blind contact an impression it is all
I bring to you all I undress

observed I learn the waste of the closed eye
how the unlit blue yields and moans

for a comet's impact the night-watchman's arrival
finally autumn acacia

the wickerwork of our promise the fine-grained wood
in the palm of your hand, embracing

my favourite poets stand at the window
a dream playing on the multi-coloured ceiling, you fall

asleep first waking time in the undergrowth
of the sheets, we plot a word

of night-time seriousness
clemency

and it doesn't last long, hardly
spring and already tired of flowering

above me the branches tie
the light in a knot letting

too little through too late to ask
for sun for more than this last

bed of wet earth and thirst
for lurking in the bud

is a hidden snare, roughly
serrated and deeply lobed

her sweet lure draws those
who dream of leaf and felt and fluff

shade-loving anemone
you come, you scarcely name me

before shadow takes the colours
or wind bends all resistance

a picking stranger sees me
in error sees moschatel

and limp snowdrops dangling
from the rigging of their roots

it's late and the hiss
stops the woman in her tracks

the hiss spies her out, assesses
the woman as suitable

under her large coat, sniping
diminutives and superlatives

diminutive diminutive superlative
furious when the woman doesn't say anything

hissing harsher coming closer
tip of his tongue point of his knife slit

more furious still
can't she even smile

pushing up against the crush barrier
of his teeth the hiss rubs

up against the bars until
excitement smothers

the hiss in his mouth
silenced through street after street

until the woman's home knowing
she's shadowed still

pond snail water lily spadderdock
bulrush dragonfly bur-reed
brown frog moorhen small fry
waterweeds diving beetles watermilfoil
duck grebe sphagnum sponge
a pair of knickers fish cat's tail
tassel stonewort fleawort starry stonewort

two red eared sliders
who dumped them here

the sunning female
absorbs the warmth
receptively cupping and stretching
her skin to the light

nearby a male
swollen throat bulging
with a bounty of worms and water plants
attracts her attention

she opens a pleat of skin on the side of her head
revealing her bright red spot, her marking, this
is the overture

she sets off slowly
below the bobbing edge of her carapace
her cloaca heaves

circumstances dictate the male gaze
because it's May

and the park lush around the pond
blue water-speedwell in flower
corolla open for fertilisation

see her
exotic
congener

under the lilac petals, tense
and blue-veined, roguish terrapin hips
dewdrops trembling on a bract

resolute and reckless
the male follows, not stumbling
over the pennywort runners

lost in the train of the yellow lines
on her buttocks, her thighs, the teasing
of the bobbing shell an unmistakable
invitation to follow

past the arum lily
through the rampant sweet flag
between the spadices, yellowish green
rising to the occasion

closer and closer

cautiously
from a premonition
because at the sound of footsteps
it's always best to
the female looks back

male thinks, 'to look
is to want', imagines
he has every right and shows the bright
red throbbing spot on his head too

unmoving

this is where the courtship begins
this is where he spreads his claws

slowly enough
his front leg
scratches

the sand, the scratched lines
extend as trembling through her throat
– the spot flushes deeper, fuller, redder

– ashamed
she shoots off, down the sloping
bank and into the water

as if it's been decided
the male dives after her
to the bottom of the pond

somewhat hindered
by the weight of his shell

while she swims in a twirling dance
manoeuvring nimbly
focussed on escape

until in one of her twirls he
with a rough thrust of his jaws
hits the back of her shell – ow

the male takes advantage of the pain
to stretch out his front legs
spread his fluttering claws

feathering, electric like the beats
of a dragonfly's wing, tingling and swelling
through her whole body

before she weakens she has to
repel the feet or are they
fins or feathers

but once again he's wrapped his claws
around her around her neck
clawing, clawing

with all her might she repels the caress
the seeing blind
might now think of an embrace

while his claws dig deeper
into her skin, under her legs, the edge of her shell

and without her wanting it
something flares up inside her
a flash of toxic pleasure

she relaxes the tension
in her hind legs

as his shell bashes brusquely
against her buttocks, the male
tries to penetrate

black and heart-shaped
his underbelly swells the member
bulging out, the monstrous protuberance

drags his lower body down
as if he's standing
on two legs, covering

her easily
despite her struggling

again and harder the lump bumps
against her shell raised
by the tickling by the force

the male hurls his black erectile
slug at her swinging
it more and more accurately

with her last resistance she shrinks
to close her opening to hide inside
herself, but, oh, the male pushes

and pounds and this time
the member sucks in tight

burns the more she writhes
the deeper he penetrates, the slug

is a screw
a dagger, how long

will the minutes last until you run out of breath
it lasts until he lets go

skin of bluish leather, the head
still virtually intact, only the right cheek
shows signs of injury the teeth
preserved in a small half-opened mouth
no trace of yelling a tuft of red hair
torn from the scalp upper body
throat and shoulders connect
relatively well – here upper body
means a bag of skin and bones –
above the left clavicle the score
of a stab wound, aberrant
vertebrae may indicate a limp
was that why the village expelled her
already harmed? in any case a smallish foot
with all toenails present and *pièce
de resistance* a complete left hand

in close proximity they found a hipbone
knee-bone, various other bones, an oak trunk
and wrapped several times around her neck
a woollen band with a slip knot, carbon-dated

the girl in the bog is approximately
two thousand years dead, sixteen years old

*After Hildegard van Bingen (1098-1179)*

to learn to speak again place a blue stone on your throat
the stone soaks the voice free from horror
the stone releases

the ailment from its syntax finally without a lump you can once again
assert how blue, deep blue the sky, how eagerly the bee, the nectar

that it is honey
in gleaming light blown violet in a fiery glow the flame
that drips from the navel and descends as a plangent sigh
leave the stone

in place long enough and the spirit too will be strengthened
against some failings against virtually all forms of anger
the stone helps

when you are lost in enthrallment
the stone will hold you tight just as you
hold the stone tight in your hand
looking back every few steps

*After Hildegard van Bingen (1098-1179)*

flame catches the sun, the peak
squeezes out burning blood oranges

rivers drip
over the scorching slope making the skin of the mountain foam

cooling night comes and obediently the water
falls below boiling point and returns to its bed

the foam sets where it lies
toughening

over three or four days under the influence of the sun
now dry and hard stones gleam in the sand
depending on the temperature and time of day
they take on different colours and active properties
they serve

good, honest purposes and are lifted up
when next the rivers flood carried
to distant lands where people gather the stones
and arrange them

in the categories abundant, incidental, rare, extremely
rare

every woman exists twice believed Praxiteles
who was so tickled by the thought
that he made two life-size sculptures
of Aphrodite

he chiselled
the goddess of love draped to her ankles
in lengthy fabric billowing at the waist

he chiselled the goddess of love without clothes for the first time
draped only in Parian marble

inconceivable in today's market but he put both statues
up for sale at the same price

the furious King of Kos demanded a discount
because dressed he considered Aphrodite dignified
and naked she was vulgar, cheap, yes, most immodest

she was banished with immediate effect to Knidos
distant city on the west coast of Asia Minor

where they placed her in the middle of an open shrine
to be circled and seen from on all sides

soon the whole empire was ablaze
and ships set sail from all of Greece

hordes of horny tourists trooped together
driven wild by the voluptuous statue's hips

even a nocturnal masturbator arrived, repeatedly
staining her breast, her thigh, her leg

overcome by pangs of regret the King of Kos
was prepared to pay off all of the city's debts
if he could acquire the disrobed goddess of love
– obviously Knidos rejected the offer

because, you see, Aphrodite wasn't just naked
but naked for the first and her nakedness was conditional
next to a body that smells and bleeds and gives birth
Praxiteles placed a pure white stone

next to her immoral appearance
the 'ameliorating circumstances'

because Aphrodite is not exposing herself, no, she's been caught
stepping out of the bath – just washed, definitely not dirty –

embarrassed she reaches for her veil already too late
to conceal herself just in time to cover

her vulva with her other hand cupped
as a shell, in this way Praxiteles

absolves the viewer of connotations
of potentially undesired bodily fluids

to be on the safe side he guides the gaze diagonally
up to two sexualised breasts

since then the sly pleasures of voyeurism
have pursued looking like an evil curse

Aphrodite still stands before that fanged eye, reduced
to the gaze that measures her availability

in depictions of the weight of the Earth
the planet is held up

for those with practical inclinations, by three wooden beams
more metaphysically they are three marble and alabaster pillars
– symbolising hope, faith and love, if it's eco-poetry

three trees, depending on who's making the claim and where in the world
oaks, spruces, olive trees, trees with holy figs, golden apple trees
wishing trees, kapok trees or a hybrid creature that looks like a tree
with the usual crown of leaves but has an alligator as a trunk

generally the Earth rests on a back
as a punishment to be borne, by Atlas for instance, down long mythologies

similarly by Chibchacum, the Muisca god of rain and thunder
who moves the globe now and then from shoulder to shoulder
causing an earthquake or the world weighs

figuratively on the shoulders of a person
with many responsibilities and worrying burdens, which leads
to absenteeism and sick notes

that's why people divvy out the carrying: supported on one side
by a mountain, on the other by a giant whose wife
stretches the sheet of the sky over the Earth, sometimes the giant takes a break
to embrace his wife, then the hemispheres shake

humankind too is said to carry the world – that's no use at all
because if humankind comes down with a fever or shivers or cries, the Earth
has the same problem, a surer bet

is relying on a team of animals
you can count on the colossal fish
with on its back a stone, and on the stone a cow that balances the globe
on one of her horns and the cow never gets neckache

or four elephants hold up the world
while standing on the back of a tortoise that's standing
on a cobra's head and everyone stays dead still to avoid quakes

or seven serpents carry the world in turn
in a tightly regulated system, this way each one
only needs to lug the Earth once every seven snakes (in their spare time
the serpents freelance as heavenly sentries, a laidback job that requires
your presence, but also provides ample opportunity
for woolgathering) in the past

people sometimes entrusted the weight of the globe
to unsuitable individuals hefty earthquakes
resulted

attributable to the sexually matured frog
who takes the world in his mouth and goes onto internet forums
to blame women for his unkissedness

hefty earthquakes

in the pocket of the playground bully
who used threats to get his hands on the blueish-green planetary marble

hefty earthquakes

caused by the speed demon whizzing
the globe along on his sled, driving his dogs through the Milky Way faster
and faster but the dogs have fleas and sometimes need to scratch

breaking a half a pomegranate in your hands
where is the knife

prising the pith out of the husk on your lap
the woman out of her tensile hide

and the fruit
flowering lips, warm-blooded, singing
itself open tremor by tremor

riders hunt through the sky, deep purple and compressed, the drumhead
sounds the dance as the skin-tight night falls – unctuous, iridescent,
we turn our bodies towards Magna Mater, Matar, Kubaba

she roars with laughter and rattles the bell ring, arranges her tall crown,
with one hand she restrains a bird of prey by gripping its beak, the other
pours wine on the soil to awaken the grapes on the vine

we play a tune to her honour on the two-snake flute
it glides through the knee-high grass it glides past our ankles and bites us
in the groin, we dance, bitten, whirling a bronze grip

around our wrists, when we feel sick from spinning
Matar holds us in the metallic pupil and warns
against the self-pollinating almond and her sweetly magnetic fruit
– press the fragrant nut to your skin and you'll fall pregnant
a wound that never heals

Matar slips the men a cutting stone
for three days and nights they must bleed under the pine

then they are given a colourful dress an inner female fire
then a procession in her honour clatters through the streets and Matar rules
without fertility symbols

she sharpens the quill and tattoos the sisters with wings
of gold leaf they chat about administrative power, the tortuous
twists of the Sakarya River, her hissing pelvis

they don't entreat her for harvests or children
they bring her a black, conical stone
a sweet fig, a pinewood staff

there are people who find it difficult to say they're tired, you say, but it's all right
for you to be tired and you moor me to the disease I've concocted, seven days
of saccharine sleep after which you pick dates from my ears, phosphorus wafts
across the oceans grains of fever kindle in new ground

you tell the fairy tale of ash and fruit
you tell me what burnt while I was asleep:
brushwood, chimneys, occupied territories

something had to burn, or else

and you're right, while I slept papaya and passionfruit
awakened in the Amazon basin from pitch-black soil, terra preta,
summoning the ash, the seed hissing full until it grows

go on, bite
the bite is butter and juice
the bite leaves a ring of charcoal around our mouths

that night I dream of a tin eagle
higher than the midday sun and wingtips
brushing the sides of the sky drowning
the field in his flapping shadow

scattering a sulphur mist from his feathers – a myriad particles, turning
the maize leaves and the manioc rind phosphorescent
present in the morning like sleep in the automatic eyes

that read in the newspapers of thirsty children
and sour mother's milk, the twisted arms of a river, over the soya fields
raptors glide through the sky on their backs, otherwise

it's spring and better, you say
to keep images of doom
like the stings of scorpions
lower than the heart

somewhere a girl starts
clapping, irrepressibly
clapping

another girl does not remain silent, a multitude of women
paint themselves with annatto and genipap
painting the cheeks of their new-born infants purple, a birth pamphlet

not him, not him
the bodily multitude demands the woman of the masses shrieks
she has brought spirits with her and through it all
the rattling maraca

call me to your bed, you say we're tired
and I can't say, I can't
start to say

which day is it today, all day the date has been erased
by fear come true, a hare shoots out of the bushes, the timid bittern
dives into the reeds

we must be watchful
or the advance of the golden jackal in the east of the country
we must report the blue-vitriol stain on the page, beneath it

are the empty streets we walk
seen from behind and there it's enough
to kick against the unfathomable gloom, a sharp elbow

in the side moodiness, you tell the story of the meerkat
that was accepted by a colony of yellow mongooses and reassure me:
lions have no interest in either species

and on days the lion bites
he's made of ink and charcoal, before saying goodbye

we'd promised each other a glimpse of wild tapirs knowing
how slim the chance, knowing tapirs
are under no obligation to us at all, but we have time

and tea biscuits and while we wait
we invent a name for the unknown tree that will blossom soon
for the first time in a thousand years

we call it 'the sleep palm feather'
while I write this down, you go on ahead in search

the spectacle ends in a confiscated circus cage
poking out between the bars, her bald, pinched muzzle
decorated here and there with a prickly tuft
as if the bear has rubbed her head on a cactus

twenty years of service have robbed her of her fur they pulled
the claws out of her paws, smashed the teeth out of her mouth
after all these years, still scared of the stick

Cholita hasn't rehearsed salvation, stage fright
when the animal rights organisation releases her
into a larger cage a sudden paradise
of fresh bales of straw and colourful blankets, finally
an extra square metre

oh, sucking hard on black grapes and ripe mango
oh, biting into juicy beets

panting with joy and well-being
Cholita looks at the camera and all over the world
animal-lovers think of the Song of Songs

they load the new, happy cage onto a truck
and after a three-day drive through the Andes
the trip continues by boat

together with other maltreated animals
Cholita motors up the Madre de Dios

when we next see her she is lying on her back
contentedly, almost like a human, in the sun

in the presumptive forest of her childhood
Cholita goes for meditative strolls
unused to the surface, she stumbles
awkwardly over branches

but there is the luxuriance
of cut fruit, the pleasure of a light anaesthetic
during the treatment of her mutilated paws

if bored she can always play a little
whack the bear-sized paper lantern swings over the pool
– all for her own fun
not the entertainment of others

to avoid nightmares the keeper hums her
the instrumental equivalent
of 'Somewhere over the Rainbow'

and gradually the music merges
with the credits:

LIFE IS WONDERFUL FOR CHOLITA, CHOLITA THE BEAR WITH NO HAIR
HAS NOT A CARE IN THE WORLD NOW

beyond the oceans
towards night
on a rocky island past her image, a woman lives
and casts off

the blue serpent locks the waterlily nipples the fang
the demented tongue sticking out
of a gaping mouth – cf. the uterus
cf. the accusations

of storytellers and mediocre heroes who
dressed her up as all kinds of

sisters temptresses trophies of war sexy monsters
victims midwives spinsters child brides, her skin

is salty and weathered
but not covered with gills
scales rust touch or scars

those who look at her
do not turn into stone she hacks
bloody coral out of rocks
lowers it wriggling into the water

an eagle ray swims
through an obstacle course of lavender applicators

a turtle gets tangled in a tampon string
dragging itself along until the end like a condemned criminal
with an absorbent ball and chain, on shore
a woman is bleeding again

down there on the reef
tattered reinforcing mesh pinions the coral skeleton

the coppery red
fades from
her paling branches

the fisherman is absent

Ilsebill has learnt
to beg empty shells for echoes of water
– she's got it down pat –

meanwhile she can drown her eyes
in memories of sounds, limp
and lacking erectile tissue

the waders hang on a hook by the door
like the stripped carcass of the spearfish
he failed

to bring home again today, hungry, waiting
she has painted her chest blue

plausible: the fisherman comes home
and hasn't been wandering, bearing excuses
and even coughing a pearl

into her innermost hand, the depths
smell of tangled sheets, of stale musty bread

the bed is a mess
where Ilsebill has been dreaming of the man with eight arms
and three hearts, in the morning she hides him

under the crumpled sea and washes
the ink stains off her thigh
all day she can't forget him

what about the pearl, the stale smell
when the fisherman comes home he will lick
her name from tentacle to tongue to lips

Ilsebill, Ilsebill

Ilsebill doesn't know why
but in his absence the fisherman has been
carrying bodies to the shore

he must have hauled them up from deep water
for they speak a briny tongue and hardly inhabit
their sparse skin, tatters, jaundiced eyes, they say
they walked with the stars until they fell into darkness

the way the sun now falls on the bodies
pressing them into their shadows

all the fisherman can do is lay
shadow upon shadow under the canvas
camping out until it dries

news: the fisherman hasn't drowned
but will extend his time at sea
in hope of catching a whale!

it's not true that the fisherman
doesn't want anyone to remind him
not the case that the passing of time makes absence and disappearance
interchangeable, sky and water equalised in darkness

as the same space with a difference in breath
he floats on the interface of the blue lung
and will not be swallowed up tonight

pursuing
sulphur bottom, deep-black bass, peerless beast

tomorrow Ilsebill will use the right knife to debeard it

given his absence the fisherman is unable
to wake her

the octopus seizes the opportunity to ask if he might
have Ilsebill's soul, keeps her pressed in the ooze of sleep, pushes
her deeper with bites

of his purple-blossoming lips there are many se se se
so many, mouth after mouth tormenting her dream se se
a briny siege

that rubs her open, waking is
reluctantly extricating herself from his tentacles

under the damp spot on the ceiling – gelatinous, pulsing
Ilsebill wants

the fisherman to know that she thought about
saying no
but when she asked what she would get in exchange
the octopus said, more and more and more and

maybe the fisherman got tangled
in the nets of a larger boat and has been
unwittingly incorporated into a corporation

three months' notice required
it would explain the duration of his absence
or why lost in an exhausted wind his voice has gradually
distorted into sighs

a constant whistling through the damp wood
of her ribcage, missing heartbeat, the waves
sworn to secrecy, cunningly

Ilsebill holds her index finger
on the border between sky and water, repeatedly
cutting herself on the sharp horizon

can the fisherman's location
be pointed out?

Ilscbill suspects the fisherman
of celebrating his absence on a remote island

on an untravelled beach
leaning on a young palm, that's how she sees him

smoking golden tobacco
beard of sand and coconut hair
Wildman, Ahab, Santiago, Robinson
leathered from skin to heart by the naked sun

and while the fisherman is lying there, lazily
caught up in distant vistas

the house is inundated submerged
to the rafters and on the floor Ilsebill
tries to find a new way to breathe

the octopus wraps all his arms around her
sticking to her like an external lung, in the morning
the air is untroubled, the floorboards dry

washed up today: a prow, rope, a seagull's leg
objects that don't necessarily decide
the fisherman's fate although his absence

is starting to take the form of his back
Ilsebill thinks about him, in not a single thought
does he turn to face her, the night light

is still expecting a silhouette the threshold too
is waiting for his wet footfall
the tinkling of the shells

but the bread turns hard and the skin on the milk
is hopelessly inflamed, under the blue paint
her chest is peeling

slowly she breaks loose, Ilsebill
makes preparations, to properly preserve
bones dip first in alcohol and shellac
then dry for three weeks

again the rasping throat-pink sound
keck-kecking seagull bark

provisional colouring
in constant transition

thrusting sweeping pulsing
the needy light attaches

without permission
to what it lets appear

the eye sinks
in the distance

in the endless
backing away